The Pencil of Nature

By

William Henry Fox Talbot

ISBN-13: 978-1721695713

ISBN-10: 1721695710

Contents

Illustrations

Introductory Remarks

The little work now presented to the Public is the first attempt to publish a series of plates or pictures wholly executed by the new art of Photogenic Drawing, without any aid whatever from the artist's pencil.

The term "Photography" is now so well known, that an explanation of it is perhaps superfluous; yet, as some persons may still be unacquainted with the art, even by name, its discovery being still of very recent date, a few words may be looked for of general explanation.

It may suffice, then, to say, that the plates of this work have been obtained by the mere action of Light upon sensitive paper. They have been formed or depicted by optical and chemical means alone, and without the aid of any one acquainted with the art of drawing. It is needless, therefore, to say that they differ in all respects, and as widely us possible, in their origin, from plates of the ordinary kind, which owe their existence to the united skill of the Artist and the Engraver.

They are impressed by Nature's hand; and what they want as yet of delicacy and finish of execution arises chiefly from our want of sufficient knowledge of her laws. When we have learnt more, by experience, respecting the formation of such pictures, they will doubtless be brought much nearer to perfection; and though we may not be able to conjecture with any certainty what rank they may hereafter attain to as pictorial productions, they will surely find their own sphere of utility, both for completeness of detail and correctness of perspective.

The Author of the present work having been so fortunate as to discover, about ten years ago, the principles and practice of Photogenic Drawing, is desirous that the first specimen of an Art, likely in all probability to be much employed in future, should be published in the country where it was first discovered. And he makes no doubt that his countrymen will deem such an intention sufficiently laudable to induce them to excuse the imperfections necessarily incident to a first attempt to exhibit an Art of so great singularity, which employs processes entirely new, and having no analogy to any thing in use before. That such imperfections will occur in a first essay, must indeed be expected. At present the Art can hardly be said to have advanced beyond its infancy—at any rate, it is yet in a very early stage—and its practice is often impeded by doubts and difficulties, which, with increasing knowledge, will diminish and disappear. Its progress will be more rapid when more minds are devoted to its improvement, and when more of skilful manual assistance is employed in the manipulation of its delicate processes; the paucity of which skilled assistance at the present moment the Author finds one of the chief difficulties in his way.

Brief Historical Sketch of the Invention of the Art

It may be proper to preface these specimens of a new Art by a brief account of the circumstances which preceded and led to the discovery of it. And these were nearly as follows.

One of the first days of the month of October 1833, I was amusing myself on the lovely shores of the Lake of Como, in Italy, taking sketches with Wollaston's Camera Lucida, or rather I should say, attempting to take them: but with the smallest possible amount of success. For when the eye was removed from the prism—in which all looked beautiful—I found that the faithless pencil had only left traces on the paper melancholy to behold.

After various fruitless attempts, I laid aside the instrument and came to the conclusion, that its use required a previous knowledge of drawing, which unfortunately I did not possess.

I then thought of trying again a method which I had tried many years before. This method was, to take a Camera Obscura, and to throw the image of the objects on a piece of transparent tracing paper laid on a pane of glass in the focus of the instrument. On this paper the objects are distinctly seen, and can be traced on it with a pencil with some degree of accuracy, though not without much time and trouble.

I had tried this simple method during former visits to Italy in 1823 and 1824, but found it in practice somewhat difficult to manage, because the pressure of the hand and pencil upon the paper tends to shake and displace the instrument (insecurely fixed, in all probability, while taking a hasty sketch by a roadside, or out of an inn window); and if the instrument is once deranged, it is most difficult to get it back again, so as to point truly in its former direction.

Besides which, there is another objection, namely, that it baffles the skill and patience of the amateur to trace all the minute details visible on the paper; so that, in fact, he carries away with him little beyond a mere souvenir of the scene—which, however, certainly has its value when looked back to, in long after years.

Such, then, was the method which I proposed to try again, and to endeavour, as before, to trace with my pencil the outlines of the scenery depicted on the paper. And this led me to reflect on the inimitable beauty of the pictures of nature's painting which the glass lens of the Camera throws upon the paper in its focus—fairy pictures, creations of a moment, and destined as rapidly to fade away.

It was during these thoughts that the idea occurred to me...how charming it would be if it were possible to cause these natural images to imprint themselves durably, and remain fixed upon the paper!

And why should it not be possible? I asked myself.

The picture, divested of the ideas which accompany it, and considered only in its ultimate nature, is but a succession or variety of stronger lights thrown upon one part of the paper, and of deeper shadows on another. Now Light, where it exists, can exert an action, and, in certain circumstances, does exert one sufficient to cause changes in material bodies. Suppose, then, such an action could be exerted on the paper; and suppose the paper could be visibly changed by it. In that case surely some effect must result having a general resemblance to the cause which produced it: so that the variegated scene of light and shade might leave its image or impression behind, stronger or weaker on different parts of the paper according to the strength or weakness of the light which had acted there.

Such was the idea that came into my mind. Whether it had ever occurred to me before amid floating philosophic visions, I know not, though I rather think it must have done so, because on this occasion it struck me so forcibly. I was then a wanderer in classic Italy, and, of course, unable to commence an inquiry of so much difficulty: but, lest the thought should again escape me between that time and my return to England, I made a careful note of it in writing, and also of such experiments as I thought would be most likely to realize it, if it were possible.

And since, according to chemical writers, the nitrate of silver is a substance peculiarly sensitive to the action of light, I resolved to make a trial of it, in the first instance, whenever occasion permitted on my return to England.

But although I knew the fact from chemical books, that nitrate of silver was changed or decomposed by Light, still I had never seen the experiment tried, and therefore I had no idea whether the action was a rapid or a slow one; a point, however, of the utmost importance, since, if it were a slow one, my theory might prove but a philosophic dream.

Such were, as nearly as I can now remember, the reflections which led me to the invention of this theory, and which first impelled me to explore a path so deeply hidden among nature's secrets. And the numerous researches which were afterwards made—whatever success may be thought to have attended them—cannot, I think, admit of a comparison with the value of the first and original idea.

In January 1834, I returned to England from my continental tour, and soon afterwards I determined to put my theories and speculations to the test of experiment, and see whether they had any real foundation.

Accordingly I began by procuring a solution of nitrate of silver, and with a brush spread some of it upon a sheet of paper, which was afterwards dried. When this paper was exposed to the sunshine, I was disappointed to find that the effect was very slowly produced in comparison with what I had anticipated.

I then tried the chloride of silver, freshly precipitated and spread upon paper while moist. This was found no better than the other, turning slowly to a darkish violet colour when exposed to the sun.

Instead of taking the chloride already formed, and spreading it upon paper, I then proceeded in the following way. The paper was first washed with a strong solution of salt, and when this was dry, it was washed again with nitrate of silver. Of course, chloride of silver was

9

thus formed in the paper, but the result of this experiment was almost the same as before, the chloride not being apparently rendered more sensitive by being formed in this way.

Similar experiments were repeated at various times, in hopes of a better result, frequently changing the proportions employed, and sometimes using the nitrate of silver before the salt, &c. &c.

In the course of these experiments, which were often rapidly performed, it sometimes happened that the brush did not pass over the whole of the paper, and of course this produced irregularity in the results. On some occasions certain portions of the paper were observed to blacken in the sunshine much more rapidly than the rest. These more sensitive portions were generally situated near the edges or confines of the part that had been washed over with the brush.

After much consideration as to the cause of this appearance, I conjectured that these bordering portions might have absorbed a lesser quantity of salt, and that, for some reason or other, this had made them more sensitive to the light. This idea was easily put to the test of experiment. A sheet of paper was moistened with a much weaker solution of salt than usual, and when dry, it was washed with nitrate of silver. This paper, when exposed to the sunshine, immediately manifested a far greater degree of sensitiveness than I had witnessed before, the whole of its surface turning black uniformly and rapidly: establishing at once and beyond all question the important fact, that a lesser quantity of salt produced a greater effect. And, as this circumstance was unexpected, it afforded a simple explanation of the cause why previous inquirers had missed this important result, in their experiments on chloride of silver, namely, because they had always operated with wrong proportions of salt and silver, using plenty of salt in order to produce a perfect chloride, whereas what was required (it was now manifest) was, to have a deficiency of salt, in order to produce an imperfect chloride, or (perhaps it should be called) a *subchloride* of silver.

So far was a free use or abundance of salt from promoting the action of light on the paper, that on the contrary it greatly weakened and almost destroyed it: so much so, that a bath of salt water was used subsequently as a fixing process to prevent the further action of light upon sensitive paper.

This process, of the formation of a subchloride by the use of a very weak solution of salt, having been discovered in the spring of 1834, no difficulty was found in obtaining distinct and very pleasing images of such things as leaves, lace, and other flat objects of complicated forms and outlines, by exposing them to the light of the sun.

The paper being well dried, the leaves, &c. were spread upon it, and covered with a glass pressed down tightly, and then placed in the sunshine; and when the paper grew dark, the whole was carried into the shade, and the objects being removed from off the paper, were found to have left their images very perfectly and beautifully impressed or delineated upon it.

But when the sensitive paper was placed in the focus of a Camera Obscura and directed to any object, as a building for instance, during a moderate space of time, as an hour or two, the effect produced upon the paper was not strong enough to exhibit such a satisfactory picture of the building as had been hoped for. The outline of the roof and of the chimneys, &c. against the sky was marked enough; but the details of the architecture were feeble, and the parts in shade were left either blank or nearly so. The sensitiveness of the paper to light, considerable as it seemed in some respects, was therefore, as yet, evidently insufficient for the purpose of obtaining pictures with the Camera Obscura; and the course of experiments had to be again renewed in hopes of attaining to some more important result.

The next interval of sufficient leisure which I found for the prosecution of this inquiry, was during a residence at Geneva in the autumn of 1834. The experiments of the previous spring were then repeated and varied in many ways; and having been struck with a remark of Sir H. Davy's which I had casually met with—that the *iodide* of silver was more sensitive to light than the *chloride,* I resolved to make trial of the iodide. Great was my surprise on making the experiment to find just the contrary of the fact alleged, and to see that the iodide was not only less sensitive than the chloride, but that it was not sensitive at all to light; indeed that it was absolutely insensible to the strongest sunshine: retaining its original tint (a pale straw colour) for any length of time unaltered in the sun. This fact showed me how little dependance was to be placed on the statements of chemical writers in regard to this particular subject, and how necessary it was to trust to nothing but actual experiment: for although there could be no doubt that Davy had observed what he described under certain circumstances—yet it was clear also, that what he had observed was some exception to the rule, and not the rule itself. In fact, further inquiry showed me that Davy must have observed a sort of subiodide in which the iodine was deficient as compared with the silver: for, as in the case of the chloride and subchloride the former is much less sensitive, so between the iodide and subiodide there is a similar contrast, but it is a much more marked and complete one.

However, the fact now discovered, proved of immediate utility; for, the iodide of silver being found to be insensible to light, and the chloride being easily converted into the iodide by immersion in iodide of potassium, it followed that a picture made with the chloride could be *fixed* by dipping it into a bath of the alkaline iodide.

This process of fixation was a simple one, and it was sometimes very successful. The disadvantages to which it was liable did not manifest themselves until a later period, and arose from a new and unexpected cause, namely, that when a picture is so treated, although it is permanently secured against the *darkening* effect of the solar rays, yet it is exposed to a contrary or *whitening* effect from them; so that after the lapse of some days the dark parts of the picture begin to fade, and gradually the whole picture becomes obliterated, and is reduced to the appearance of a uniform pale yellow sheet of paper.

A good many pictures, no doubt, escape this fate, but as they all seem liable to it, the fixing process by iodine must be considered as not sufficiently certain to be retained in use as a photographic process, except when employed with several careful precautions which it would be too long to speak of in this place.

During the brilliant summer of 1835 in England I made new attempts to obtain pictures of buildings with the Camera Obscura; and having devised a process which gave additional sensibility to the paper, viz. by giving it repeated alternate washes of salt and silver, and using it in a moist state, I succeeded in reducing the time necessary for obtaining an image with the Camera Obscura on a bright day to ten minutes. But these pictures, though very pretty, were very small, being quite miniatures. Some were obtained of a larger size, but they required much patience, nor did they seem so perfect as the smaller ones, for it was difficult to keep the instrument steady for a great length of time pointing at the same object, and the paper being used moist was often acted on irregularly.

During the three following years not much was added to previous knowledge. Want of sufficient leisure for experiments was a great obstacle and hindrance, and I almost resolved to publish some account of the Art in the imperfect state in which it then was.

However curious the results which I had met with, yet I felt convinced that much more important things must remain behind, and that the clue was still wanting to this labyrinth of facts. But as there seemed no immediate prospect of further success, I thought of drawing up a short account of what had been done, and presenting it to the Royal Society.

However, at the close of the year 1838, I discovered a remarkable fact of quite a new kind. Having spread a piece of silver leaf on a pane of glass, and thrown a particle of iodine upon it, I observed that coloured rings formed themselves around the central particle, especially if the glass was slightly warmed. The coloured rings I had no difficulty in attributing to the formation of infinitely thin layers or strata of iodide of silver; but a most unexpected phenomenon occurred when the silver plate was brought into the light by placing it near a window. For then the coloured rings shortly began to change their colours, and assumed other and quite unusual tints, such as are never seen in the *"colours of thin plates."* For instance, the part of the silver plate which at first shone with a pale yellow colour, was changed to a dark olive green when brought into the daylight. This change was not very rapid: it was much less rapid than the changes of some of the sensitive papers which I had been in the habit of employing, and therefore, after having admired the beauty of this new phenomenon, I laid the specimens by, for a time, to see whether they would preserve the same appearance, or would undergo any further alteration.

Such was the progress which I had made in this inquiry at the close of the year 1838, when an event occurred in the scientific world, which in some degree frustrated the hope with which I had pursued, during nearly five years, this long and complicated, but interesting series of experiments—the hope, namely, of being the first to announce to the world the existence of the New Art—which has been since named Photography.

I allude, of course, to the publication in the mouth of January 1839, of the great discovery of M. Daguerre, of the photographic process which he has called the Daguerreotype. I need not speak of the sensation created in all parts of the world by the first announcement of this splendid discovery, or rather, of the fact of its having been made, (for the actual method made use of was kept secret for many months longer). This great and sudden celebrity was due to two causes: first, to the beauty of the discovery itself: secondly, to the zeal and enthusiasm of Arago, whose eloquence, animated by private friendship, delighted in extolling the inventor of this new art, sometimes to the assembled science of the French Academy, at other times to the less scientific judgment, but not less eager patriotism, of the Chamber of Deputies.

But, having brought this brief notice of the early days of the Photographic Art to the important epoch of the announcement of the Daguerreotype, I shall defer the subsequent history of the Art to a future number of this work.

Some time previously to the period of which I have now been speaking, I met with an account of some researches on the action of Light, by Wedgwood and Sir H. Davy, which, until then, I had never heard of. Their short memoir on this subject was published in 1802 in the first volume of the Journal of the Royal Institution. It is curious and interesting, and certainly establishes their claim as the first inventors of the Photographic Art, though the actual progress they made in it was small. They succeeded, indeed, in obtaining impressions from solar light of flat objects laid upon a sheet of prepared paper, but they say that they found it impossible to fix or preserve those pictures: all their numerous attempts to do so having failed.

And with respect to the principal branch of the Art, viz. the taking pictures of distant objects with a Camera Obscura, they attempted to do so, but obtained no result at all, however long the experiment lasted. While therefore due praise should be awarded to them for making the attempt, they have no claim to the actual discovery of any process by which such a picture can really be obtained.

It is remarkable that the failure in this respect appeared so complete, that the subject was soon after abandoned both by themselves and others, and as far as we can find, it was never resumed again. The thing fell into entire oblivion for more than thirty years: and therefore, though the Daguerreotype was not so entirely new a conception as M. Daguerre and the French Institute imagined, and though my own labours had been still more directly anticipated by Wedgwood, yet the improvements were so great in all respects, that I think the year 1839 may fairly be considered as the real date of birth of the Photographic Art, that is to say, its first public disclosure to the world.

There is a point to which I wish to advert, which respects the execution of the following specimens. As far as respects the design, the copies are almost facsimiles of each other, but there is some variety in the tint which they present. This arises from a twofold cause. In the first place, each picture is separately formed by the light of the sun, and in our climate the strength of the sun's rays is exceedingly variable even in serene weather. When clouds intervene, a longer time is of course allowed for the impression of a picture, but it is not possible to reduce this to a matter of strict and accurate calculation.

The other cause is the variable quality of the paper employed, even when furnished by the same manufacturers—some differences in the fabrication and in the *sizing* of the paper, known only to themselves, and perhaps secrets of the trade, have a considerable influence on the tone of colour which the picture ultimately assumes.

These tints, however, might undoubtedly be brought nearer to uniformity, if any great advantage appeared likely to result: but, several persons of taste having been consulted on the point, viz. which tint on the whole deserved a preference, it was found that their opinions offered nothing approaching to unanimity, and therefore, as the process presents us spontaneously with a variety of shades of colour, it was thought best to admit whichever appeared pleasing to the eye, without aiming at an uniformity which is hardly attainable. And with these brief observations I commend the pictures to the indulgence of the Gentle Reader.

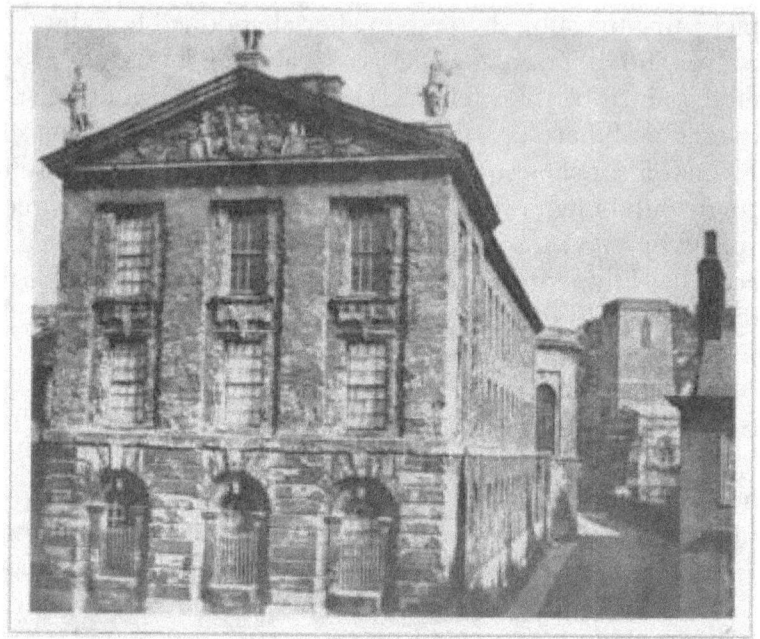

PLATE I. PART OF QUEEN'S COLLEGE, OXFORD.

This building presents on its surface the most evident marks of the injuries of time and weather, in the abraded state of the stone, which probably was of a bad quality originally.

The view is taken from the other side of the High Street—looking North. The time is morning.

In the distance is seen at the end of a narrow street the Church of St. Peter's in the East, said to be the most ancient church in Oxford, and built during the Saxon era. This street, shortly after passing the church, turns to the left, and leads to New College.

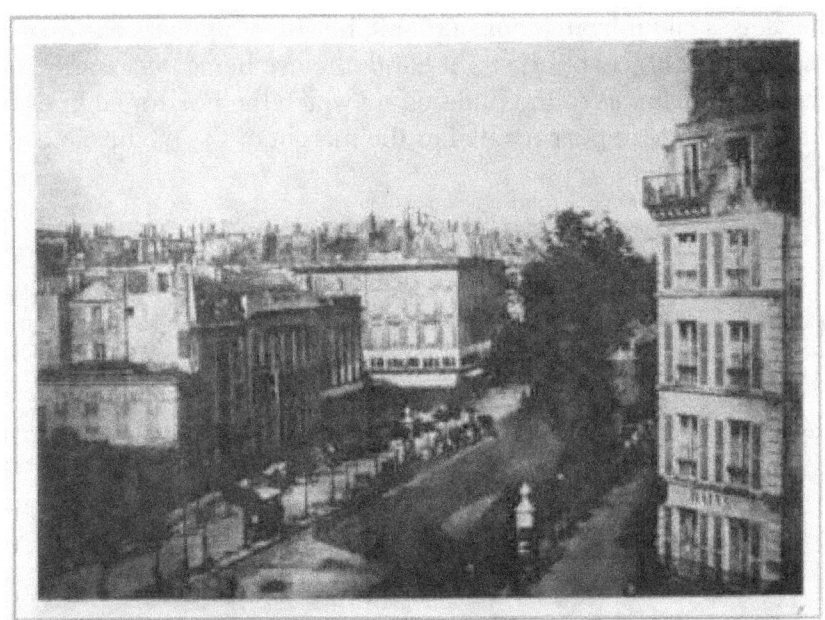

PLATE II. VIEW OF THE BOULEVARDS AT PARIS.

This view was taken from one of the upper windows of the Hotel de Douvres, situated at the corner of the Rue de la Paix. The spectator is looking to the North-east. The time is the afternoon. The sun is just quitting the range of buildings adorned with columns: its façade is already in the shade, but a single shutter standing open projects far enough forward to catch a gleam of sunshine. The weather is hot and dusty, and they have just been watering the road, which has produced two broad bands of shade upon it, which unite in the foreground, because, the road being partially under repair (as is seen from the two wheelbarrows, &c. &c.), the watering machines have been compelled to cross to the other side.

By the roadside a row of *cittadines* and cabriolets are waiting, and a single carriage stands in the distance a long way to the right.

A whole forest of chimneys borders the horizon: for, the instrument chronicles whatever it sees, and certainly would delineate a chimney-pot or a chimney-sweeper with the same impartiality as it would the Apollo of Belvedere.

The view is taken from a considerable height, as appears easily by observing the house on the right hand; the eye being necessarily on a level with that part of the building on which the horizontal lines or courses of stone appear parallel to the margin of the picture.

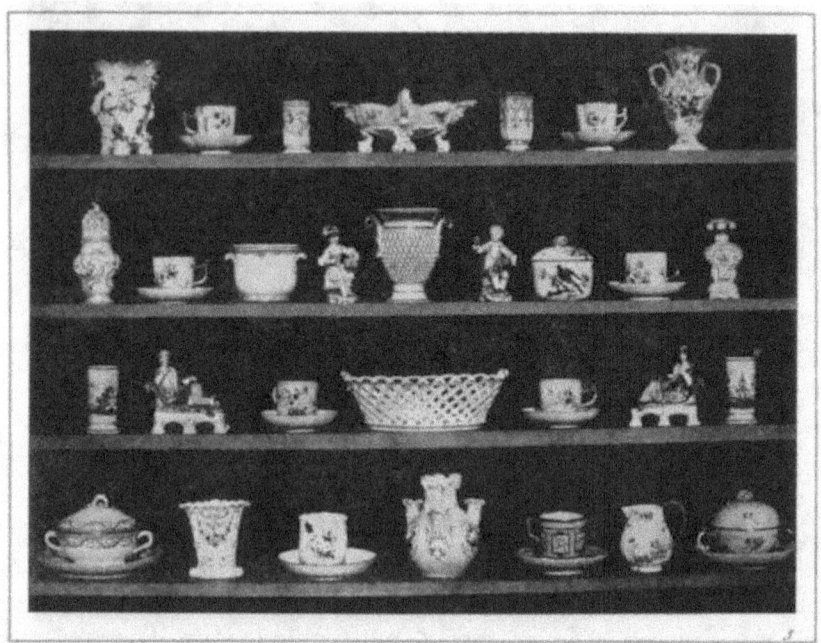

PLATE III. ARTICLES OF CHINA.

From the specimen here given it is sufficiently manifest, that the whole cabinet of a Virtuoso and collector of old China might be depicted on paper in little more time than it would take him to make a written inventory describing it in the usual way. The more strange and fantastic the forms of his old teapots, the more advantage in having their pictures given instead of their descriptions.

And should a thief afterwards purloin the treasures—if the mute testimony of the picture were to be produced against him in court—it would certainly be evidence of a novel kind; but what the judge and jury might say to it, is a matter which I leave to the speculation of those who possess legal acumen.

The articles represented on this plate are numerous: but, however numerous the objects—however complicated the arrangement—the

18

Camera depicts them all at once. It may be said to make a picture of whatever *it sees.* The object glass is the *eye* of the instrument—the sensitive paper may be compared to the *retina.* And, the eye should not have too large a *pupil:* that is to say, the glass should be diminished by placing a screen or diaphragm before it, having a small circular hole, through which alone the rays of light may pass. When the eye of the instrument is made to look at the objects through this contracted aperture, the resulting image is much more sharp and correct. But it takes a longer time to impress itself upon the paper, because, in proportion as the aperture is contracted, fewer rays enter the instrument from the surrounding objects, and consequently fewer fall upon each part of the paper.

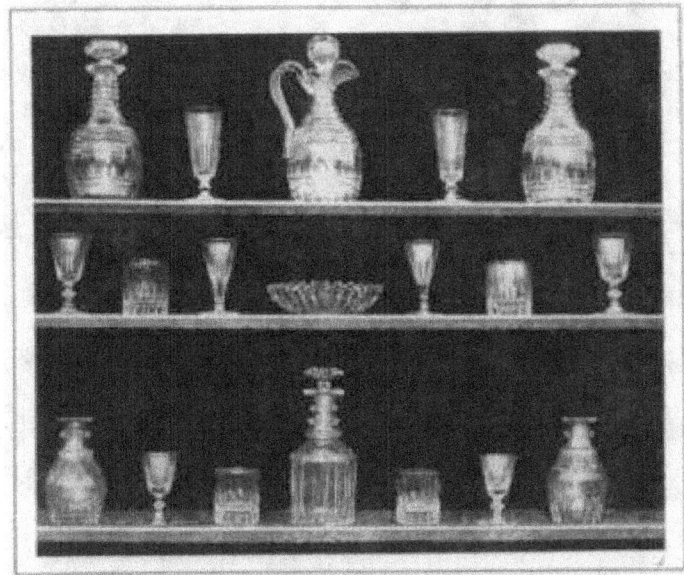

PLATE IV. ARTICLES OF GLASS.

The photogenic images of glass articles impress the sensitive paper with a very peculiar touch, which is quite different from that of the China in Plate III. And it may be remarked that white china and glass do not succeed well when represented together, because the picture of the china, from its superior brightness, is completed before that of the glass is well begun. But coloured china may be introduced along with glass in the same picture, provided the colour is not a pure blue: since blue objects affect the sensitive paper almost as rapidly as white ones do. On the contrary, green rays act very feebly—an inconvenient circumstance, whenever green trees are to be represented in the same picture with buildings of a light hue, or with any other light coloured objects.

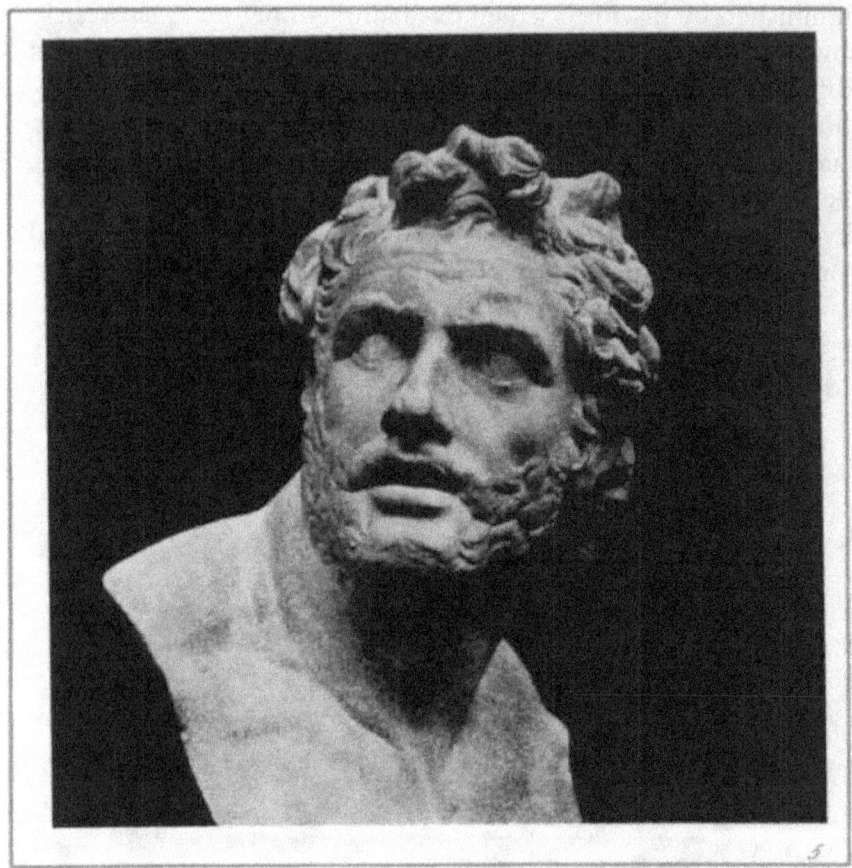

PLATE V. BUST OF PATROCLUS.

Statues, busts, and other specimens of sculpture, are generally well represented by the Photographic Art; and also very rapidly, in consequence of their whiteness.

These delineations are susceptible of an almost unlimited variety: since in the first place, a statue may be placed in any position with regard to the sun, either directly opposite to it, or at any angle: the directness or obliquity of the illumination causing of course an immense difference in the effect. And when a choice has been made

20

of the direction in which the sun's rays shall fall, the statue may be then turned round on its pedestal, which produces a second set of variations no less considerable than the first. And when to this is added the change of size which is produced in the image by bringing the Camera Obscura nearer to the statue or removing it further off, it becomes evident how very great a number of different effects may be obtained from a single specimen of sculpture.

With regard to many statues, however, a better effect is obtained by delineating them in cloudy weather than in sunshine. For, the sunshine causes such strong shadows as sometimes to confuse the subject. To prevent this, it is a good plan to hold a white cloth on one side of the statue at a little distance to reflect back the sun's rays and cause a faint illumination of the parts which would otherwise be lost in shadow.

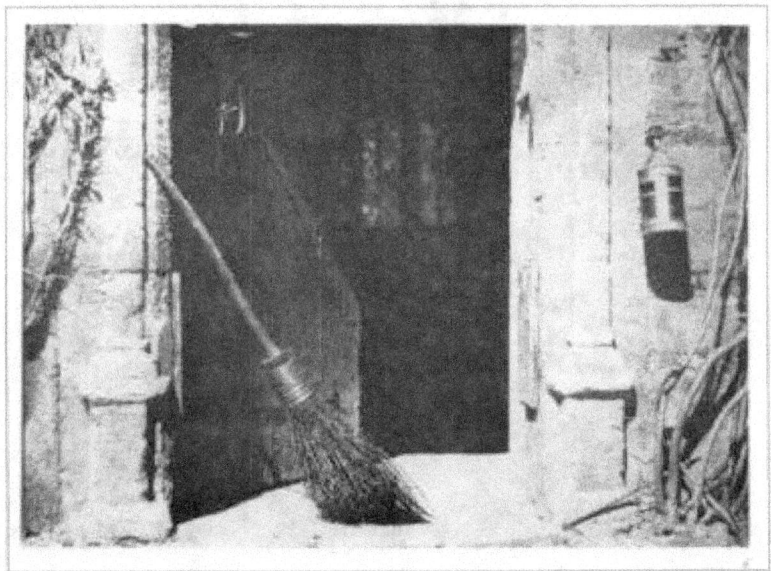

PLATE VI. THE OPEN DOOR.

The chief object of the present work is to place on record some of the early beginnings of a new art, before the period, which we trust is approaching, of its being brought to maturity by the aid of British talent.

This is one of the trifling efforts of its infancy, which some partial friends have been kind enough to commend.

We have sufficient authority in the Dutch school of art, for taking as subjects of representation scenes of daily and familiar occurrence. A painter's eye will often be arrested where ordinary people see nothing remarkable. A casual gleam of sunshine, or a shadow thrown across his path, a time-withered oak, or a moss-covered stone may awaken a train of thoughts and feelings, and picturesque imaginings.

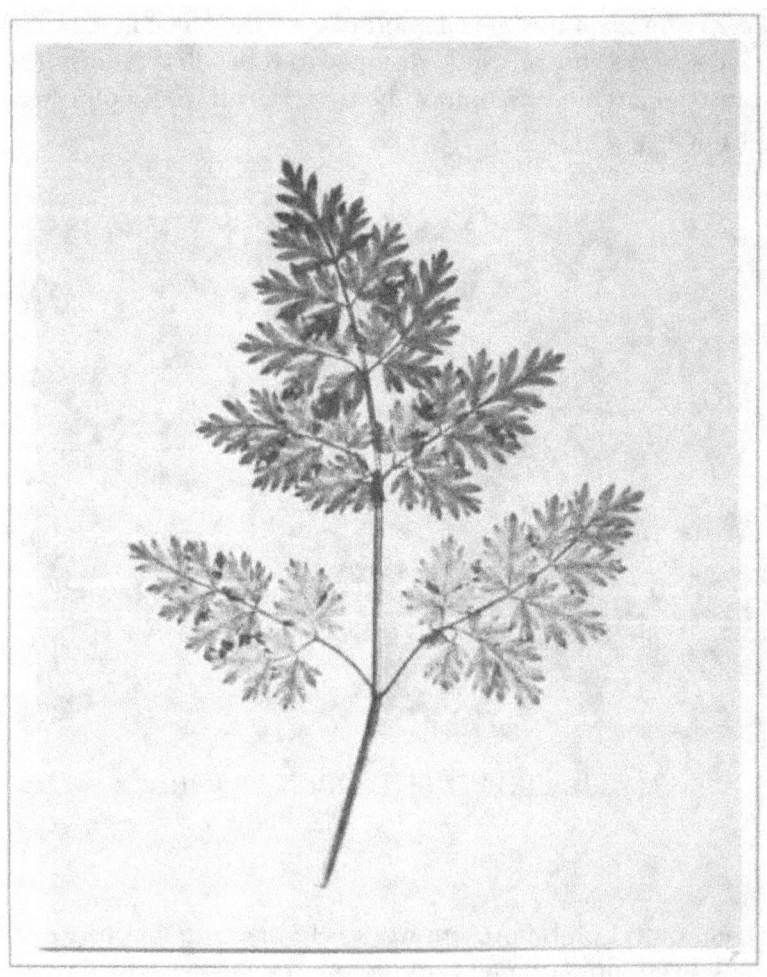

PLATE VII. LEAF OF A PLANT.

Hitherto we have presented to the reader the representations of distant objects, obtained by the use of a Camera Obscura. But the present plate represents an object of its natural size. And this is effected by quite a different and much simpler process, as follows.

A leaf of a plant, or any similar object which is thin and delicate, is laid flat upon a sheet of prepared paper which is moderately sensitive. It is then covered with a glass, which is pressed down tight upon it by means of screws.

This done, it is placed in the sunshine for a few minutes, until the exposed parts of the paper have turned dark brown or nearly black. It is then removed into a shady place, and when the leaf is taken up, it is found to have left its impression or picture on the paper. This image is of a pale brown tint if the leaf is semi-transparent, or it is quite white if the leaf is opaque.

The leaves of plants thus represented in white upon a dark background, make very pleasing pictures, and I shall probably introduce a few specimens of them in the sequel of this work: but the present plate shews one pictured in the contrary manner, viz. dark upon a white ground: or, speaking in the language of photography, it is a *positive* and not a *negative* image of it. The change is accomplished by simply repeating the first process. For, that process, as above described, gives a white image on a darkened sheet of paper: this sheet is then taken and washed with a fixing liquid to destroy the sensibility of the paper and fix the image on it.

This done, the paper is dried, and then it is laid upon a second sheet of sensitive paper, being pressed into close contact with it, and placed in the sunshine: this second process is evidently only a repetition of the first. When, finished, the second paper is found to have received an image of a contrary kind to the first; the ground being white, and the image upon it dark.

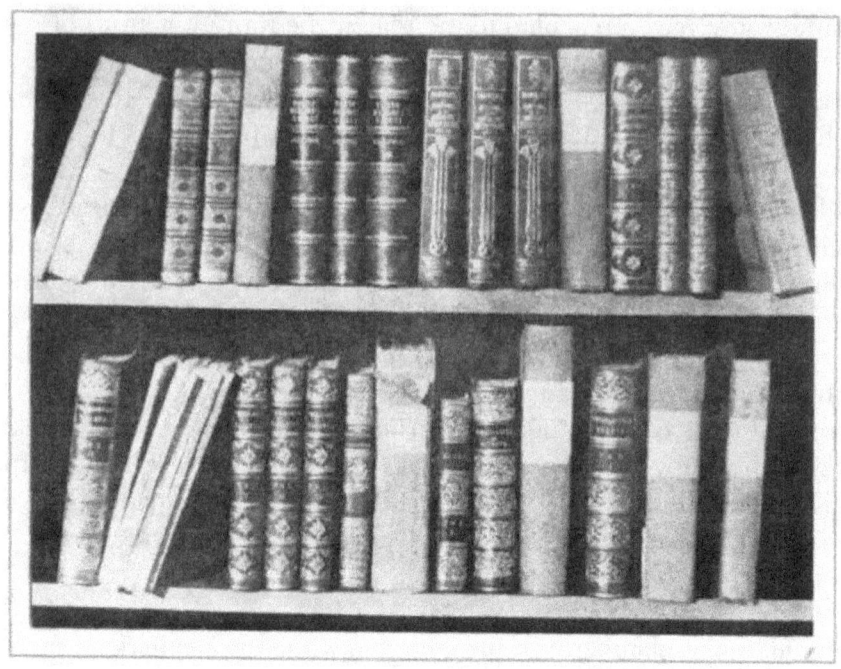

PLATE VIII. A SCENE IN A LIBRARY.

Among the many novel ideas which the discovery of Photography
has suggested, is the following rather curious experiment or
speculation. I have never tried it, indeed, nor am I aware that any
one else has either tried or proposed it, yet I think it is one which, if
properly managed, must inevitably succeed.

When a ray of solar light is refracted by a prism and thrown upon a
screen, it forms there the very beautiful coloured band known by
the name of the solar spectrum.

Experimenters have found that if this spectrum is thrown upon a
sheet of sensitive paper, the violet end of it produces the principal
effect: and, what is truly remarkable, a similar effect is produced by
certain *invisible rays* which lie beyond the violet, and beyond the
limits of the spectrum, and whose existence is only revealed to us by
this action which they exert.

Now, I would propose to separate these invisible rays from the rest,
by suffering them to pass into an adjoining apartment through an

24

aperture in a wall or screen of partition. This apartment would thus become filled (we must not call it *illuminated)* with invisible rays, which might be scattered in all directions by a convex lens placed behind the aperture. If there were a number of persons in the room, no one would see the other: and yet nevertheless if a *camera* were so placed as to point in the direction in which any one were standing, it would take his portrait, and reveal his actions.

For, to use a metaphor we have already employed, the eye of the camera would see plainly where the human eye would find nothing but darkness.

Alas! that this speculation is somewhat too refined to be introduced with effect into a modern novel or romance; for what a *dénouement* we should have, if we could suppose the secrets of the darkened chamber to be revealed by the testimony of the imprinted paper.

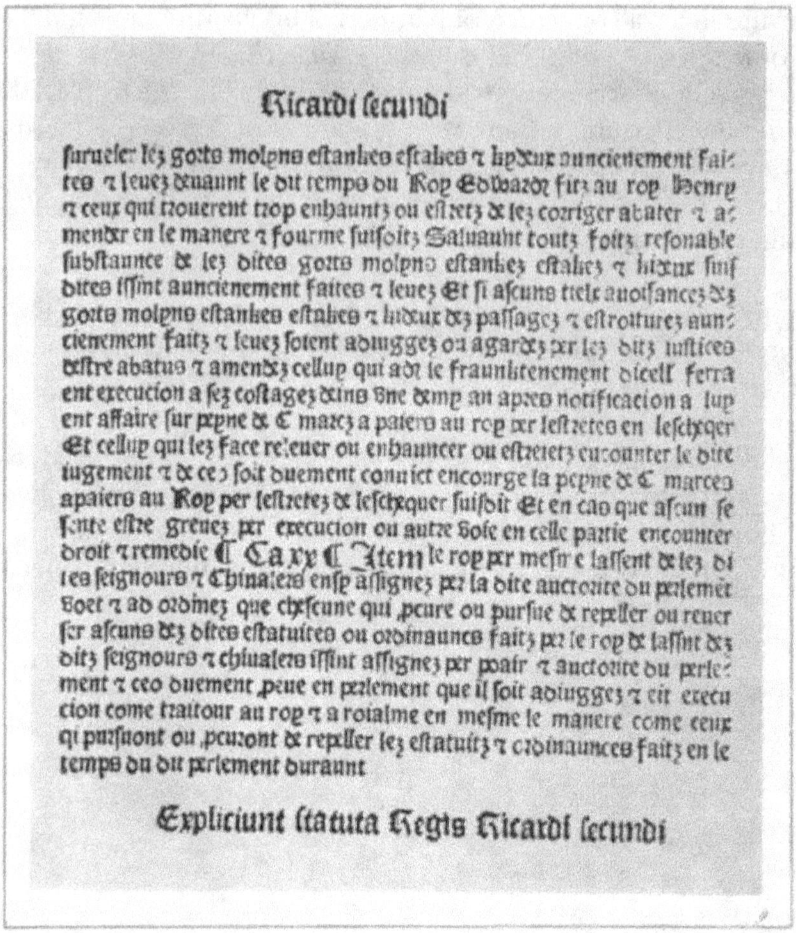

PLATE IX. FAC-SIMILE OF AN OLD PRINTED PAGE.

Taken from a black-letter volume in the Author's library, containing the statutes of Richard the Second, written in Norman French. To the Antiquarian this application of the photographic art seems destined to be of great advantage.

Copied of the size of the original, by the method of superposition.

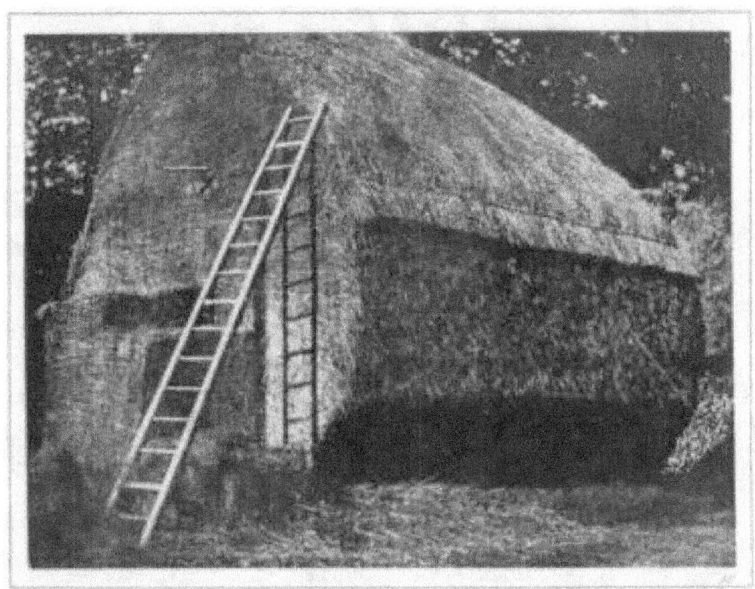

PLATE X. THE HAYSTACK.

One advantage of the discovery of the Photographic Art will be, that it will enable us to introduce into our pictures a multitude of minute details which add to the truth and reality of the representation, but which no artist would take the trouble to copy faithfully from nature.

Contenting himself with a general effect, he would probably deem it beneath his genius to copy every accident of light and shade; nor could he do so indeed, without a disproportionate expenditure of time and trouble, which might be otherwise much better employed.

Nevertheless, it is well to have the means at our disposal of introducing these minutiæ without any additional trouble, for they will sometimes be found to give an air of variety beyond expectation to the scene represented.

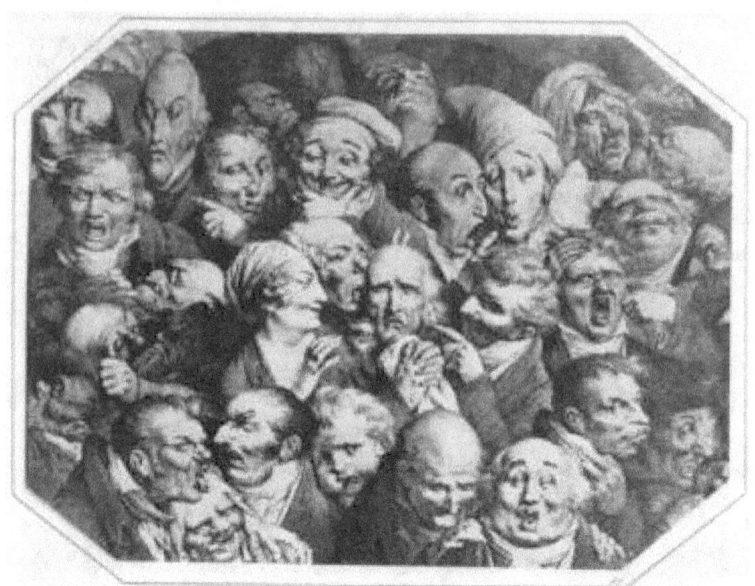

PLATE XI. COPY OF A LITHOGRAPHIC PRINT.

We have here the copy of a Parisian caricature, which is probably
well known to many of my readers. All kinds of engravings may be
copied by photographic means; and this application of the art is a
very important one, not only as producing in general nearly fac-
simile copies, but because it enables us at pleasure to alter the scale,
and to make the copies as much larger or smaller than the originals
as we may desire.

The old method of altering the size of a design by means of a
pantagraph or some similar contrivance, was very tedious, and must
have required the instrument to be well constructed and kept in very
excellent order: whereas the photographic copies become larger or
smaller, merely by placing the originals nearer to or farther from the
Camera.

The present plate is an example of this useful application of the art,
being a copy greatly diminished in size, yet preserving all the
proportions of the original.

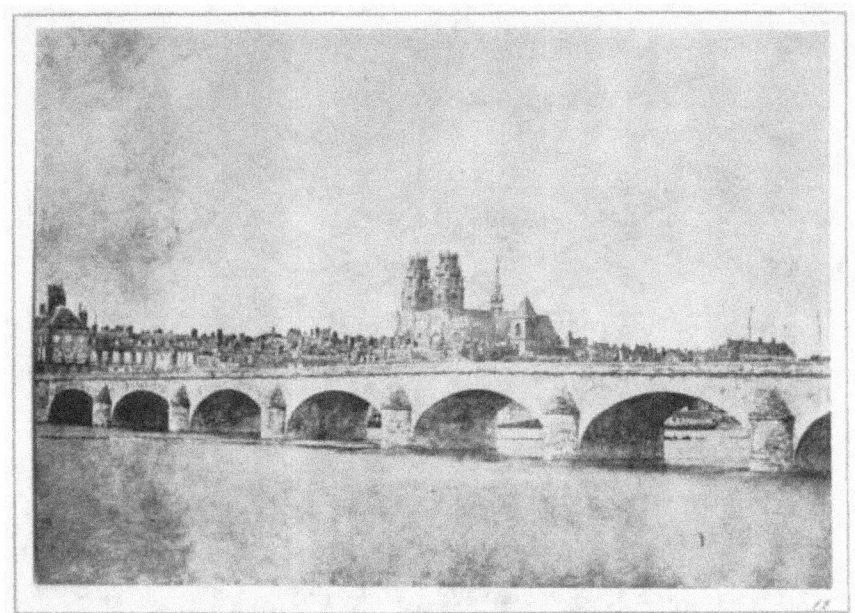

PLATE XII. THE BRIDGE OF ORLEANS.

This view is taken from the southern bank of the river Loire, which passes Orleans in a noble stream.

A city rich in historical recollections, but at present chiefly interesting from its fine Cathedral; of which I hope to give a representation in a subsequent plate of this work.

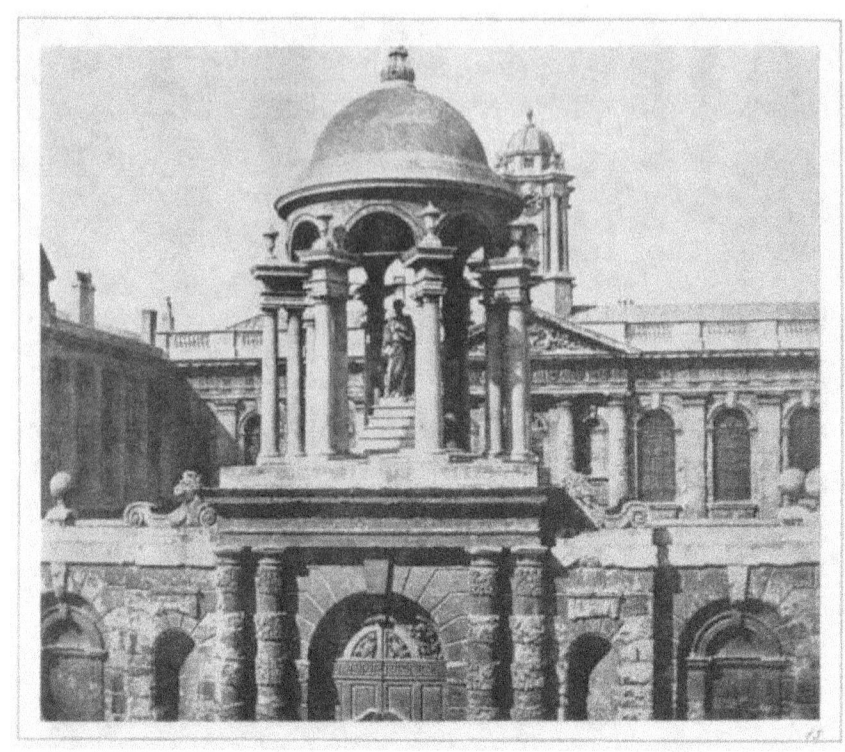

PLATE XIII. QUEEN'S COLLEGE, OXFORD, Entrance
Gateway

ENTRANCE GATEWAY.

In the first plate of this work I have represented an angle of this building. Here we have a view of the Gateway and central portion of the College. It was taken from a window on the opposite side of the High Street. In examining photographic pictures of a certain degree of perfection, the use of a large lens is recommended, such as elderly persons frequently employ in reading. This magnifies the objects two or three times, and often discloses a multitude of minute details, which were previously unobserved and unsuspected. It frequently happens, moreover—and this is one of the charms of photography—that the operator himself discovers on examination, perhaps long afterwards, that he has depicted many things he had no notion of at the time. Sometimes inscriptions and dates are found upon the buildings, or printed placards most irrelevant, are discovered upon their walls: sometimes a distant dial-plate is seen, and upon it—unconsciously recorded—the hour of the day at which the view was taken.

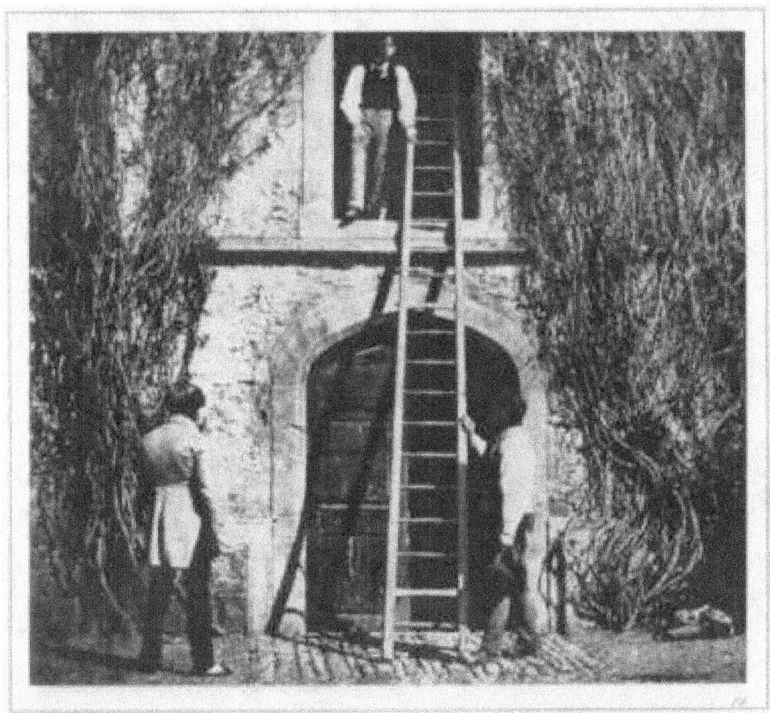

PLATE XIV. THE LADDER.

Portraits of living persons and groups of figures form one of the most attractive subjects of photography, and I hope to present some of them to the Reader in the progress of the present work.

When the sun shines, small portraits can be obtained by my process in one or two seconds, but large portraits require a somewhat longer time. When the weather is dark and cloudy, a corresponding allowance is necessary, and a greater demand is made upon the patience of the sitter. Groups of figures take no longer time to obtain than single figures would require, since the Camera depicts them all at once, however numerous they may be: but at present we cannot well succeed in this branch of the art without some previous concert and arrangement. If we proceed to the City, and attempt to take a picture of the moving multitude, we fail, for in a small fraction of a second they change their positions so much, as to destroy the distinctness of the representation. But when a group of persons has been artistically arranged, and trained by a little practice to maintain an absolute immobility for a few seconds of time, very delightful pictures are easily obtained. I have observed that family groups are especial favourites: and the same five or six individuals may be combined in so many varying attitudes, as to give much interest and a great air of reality to a series of such pictures. What would not be the value to our English Nobility of such a record of their ancestors who lived a century ago? On how small a portion of their family picture galleries can they really rely with confidence!

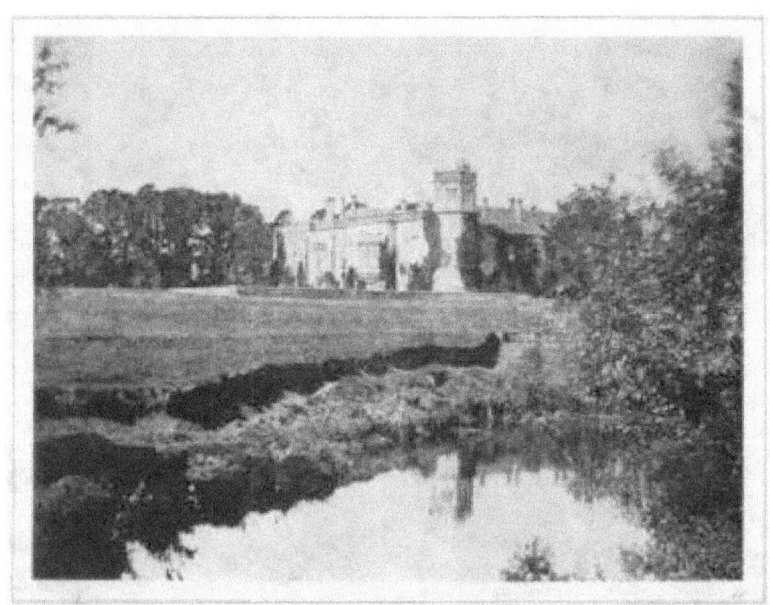

PLATE XV. LACOCK ABBEY IN WILTSHIRE.

One of a series of views representing the Author's country seat in Wiltshire. It is a religious structure of great antiquity, erected early in the thirteenth century, many parts of which are still remaining in excellent preservation. This plate gives a distant view of the Abbey, which is seen reflected in the waters of the river Avon. The spectator is looking to the North West.

The tower which occupies the South-eastern corner of the building is believed to be of Queen Elizabeth's time, but the lower portion of it is much older, and coeval with the first foundation of the abbey.

In my first account of "The Art of Photogenic Drawing," read to the Royal Society in January, 1839, I mentioned this building as being the first "that was ever yet known to have drawn its own picture."

It was in the summer of 1835 that these curious self-representations were first obtained. Their size was very small: indeed, they were but miniatures, though very distinct: and the shortest time of making them was nine or ten minutes.

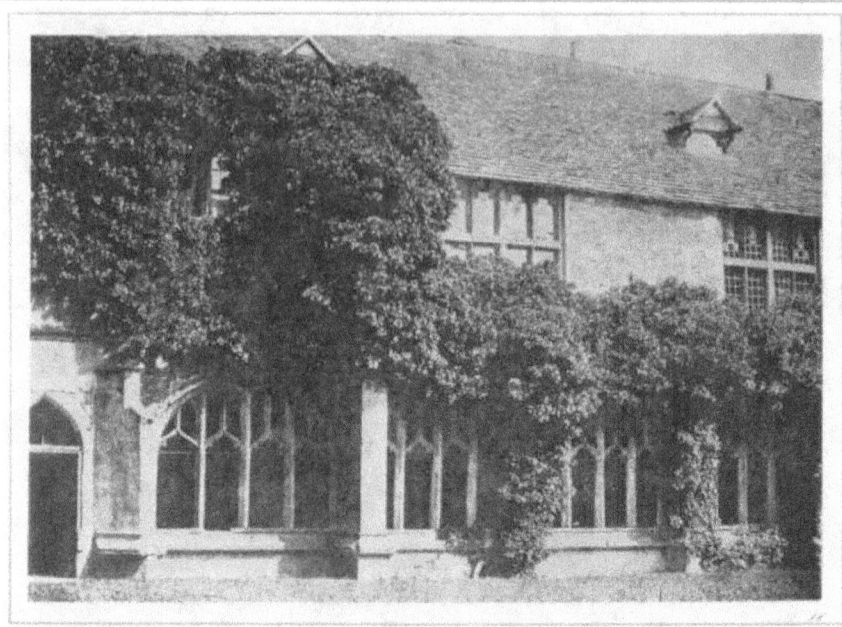

PLATE XVI. CLOISTERS OF LACOCK ABBEY.

The Abbey was founded by Ela, Countess of Salisbury, widow of William Longspee, son of King Henry II. and Fair Rosamond.

This event took place in the year of our Lord 1229, in the reign of Henry III. She was elected to be the first abbess, and ruled for many years with prudence and piety. She lies buried in the cloisters, and this inscription is read upon her tomb:

Infrà sunt defossa Elæ venerabilis ossa,
Quæ dedit has sedes sacras monialibus ædes,
Abbatissa quidem quæ sanctè vixit ibidem,
Et comitissa Sarum virtutum plena bonarum:

The cloisters, however, in their present state, are believed to be of the time of Henry VI. They range round three sides of a quadrangle, and are the most perfect which remain in any private residence in England. By moonlight, especially, their effect is very picturesque and solemn.

Here, I presume, the holy sisterhood often paced in silent meditation; though, in truth, they have left but few records to posterity to tell us how they lived and died. The "liber de Lacock" is supposed to have perished in the fire of the Cottonian library. What it contained I know not—perhaps their private memoirs. Some things, however, have been preserved by tradition, or discovered by the zeal of antiquaries, and from these materials the poet Bowles has composed an interesting work, the History of Lacock Abbey, which he published in 1835.

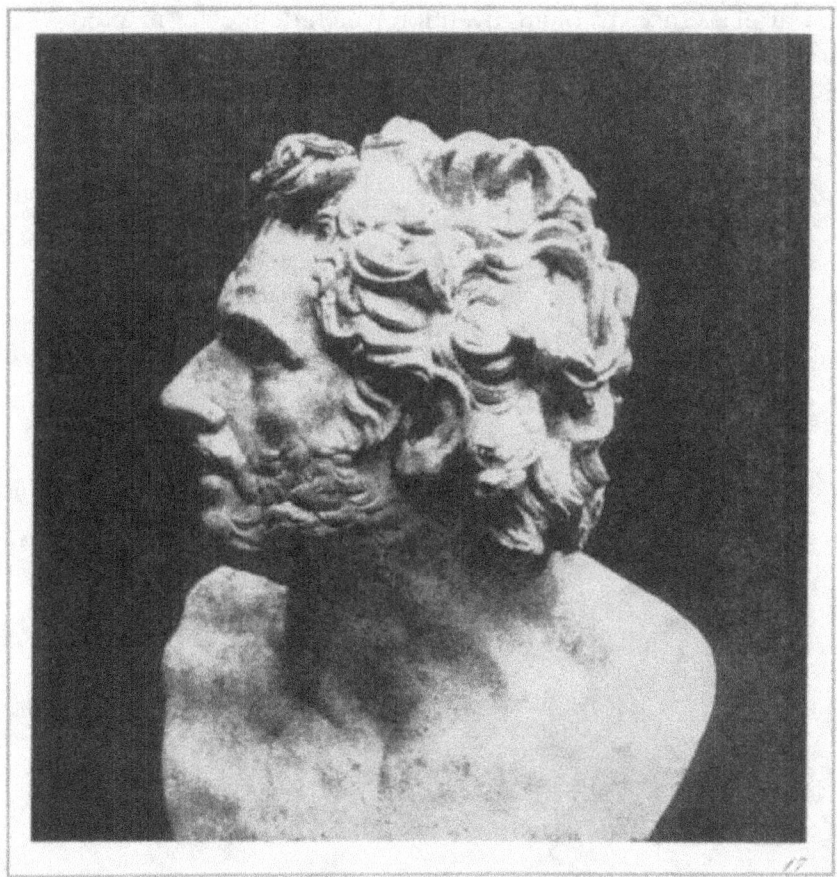

PLATE XVII. BUST OF PATROCLUS.

Another view of the bust which figures in the fifth plate of this work.

35

Is has often been said, and has grown into a proverb, that there is no royal road to learning of any kind. But the proverb is fallacious: for there is, assuredly, a royal road to *Drawing*, and one of these days, when more known and better explored, it will probably be much frequented. Already sundry *amateurs* have laid down the pencil and armed themselves with chemical solutions and with *camera obscuræ.* Those amateurs especially, and they are not few, who find the rules of *perspective* difficult to learn and to apply—and who moreover have the misfortune to be lazy—prefer to use a method which dispenses with all that trouble. And even accomplished artists now avail themselves of an invention which delineates in a few moments the almost endless details of Gothic architecture which a whole day would hardly suffice to draw correctly in the ordinary manner.

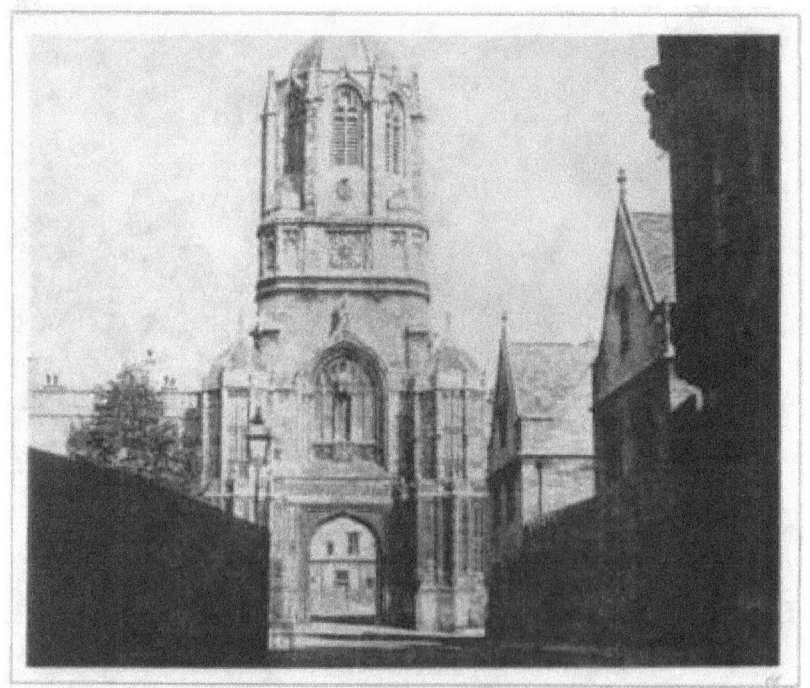

PLATE XVIII. GATE OF CHRISTCHURCH.

The principal gate of Christchurch College in the University of Oxford.

On the right of the picture are seen the buildings of Pembroke College in shade.

Those who have visited Oxford and Cambridge in vacation time in the summer must have been struck with the silence and tranquillity which pervade those venerable abodes of learning.

Those ancient courts and quadrangles and cloisters look so beautiful so tranquil and so solemn at the close of a summer's evening, that the spectator almost thinks he gazes upon a city of former ages, deserted, but not in ruins: abandoned by man, but spared by Time. No other cities in Great Britain awake feelings at all similar. In other towns you hear at all times the busy hum of passing crowds, intent on traffic or on pleasure—but Oxford in the summer season seems the dwelling of the Genius of Repose.

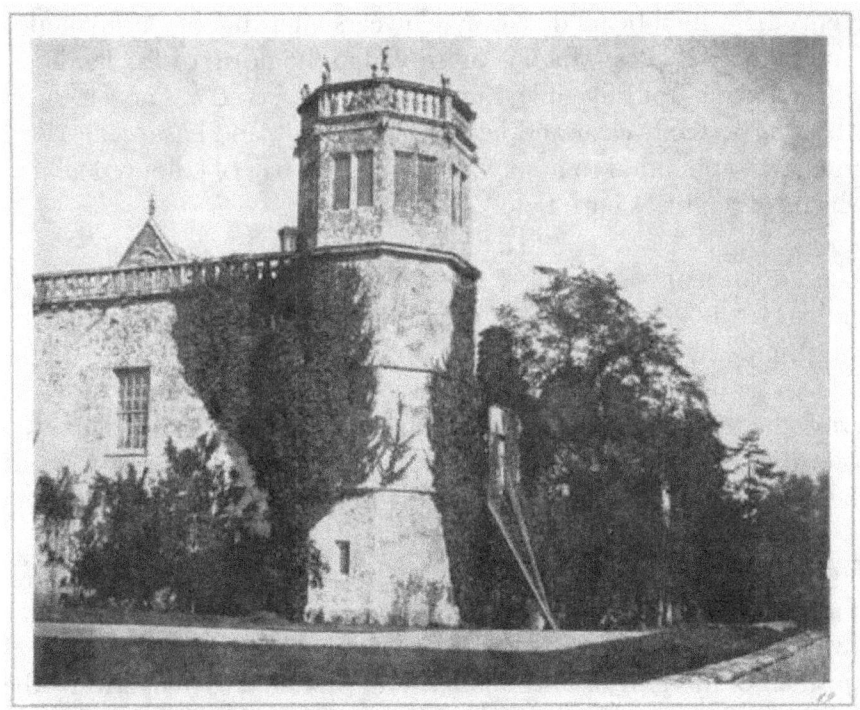

PLATE XIX. THE TOWER OF LACOCK ABBEY

The upper part of the tower is believed to be of Queen Elizabeth's time, but the lower part is probably coeval with the first foundation of the abbey, in the reign of Henry III.

The tower contains three apartments, one in each story. In the central one, which is used as a muniment room, there is preserved an invaluable curiosity, an original copy of the Magna Charta of King Henry III. It appears that a copy of this Great Charter was sent to the sheriffs of all the counties in England. The illustrious Ela, Countess of Salisbury, was at that time sheriff of Wiltshire (at least so tradition confidently avers), and this was the copy transmitted to her, and carefully preserved ever since her days in the abbey which she founded about four years after the date of this Great Charter.

Of the Magna Charta of King John several copies are still extant; but only two copies are known to exist of the Charter of his successor Henry III, which bears date only ten years after that of Runnymede. One of these copies, which is preserved in the north of England, is defaced and wholly illegible; but the copy preserved at Lacock Abbey is perfectly clear and legible throughout, and has a seal of green wax appended to it, inclosed in a small bag of coloured silk, which six centuries have faded.

The Lacock copy is therefore the only authority from which the text of this Great Charter can be correctly known; and from this copy it was printed by Blackstone, as he himself informs us.

From the top of the tower there is an extensive view, especially towards the South, where the eye ranges as far as Alfred's Tower, in the park of Stour-head, about twenty-three miles distant.

From the parapet wall of this building, three centuries ago, Olive Sherington, the heiress of Lacock, threw herself into the arms of her lover, a gallant gentleman of Worcestershire, John Talbot, a kinsman of the Earl of Shrewsbury. He was felled to the earth by the blow, and for a time lay lifeless, while the lady only wounded or broke her finger. Upon this, Sir Henry Sherington, her father, relented, and shortly after consented to their marriage, giving as a reason *"the step which his daughter had taken."*

Unwritten tradition in many families has preserved ancient stories which border on the marvellous, and it may have embellished the tale of this lover's leap by an incident belonging to another age. For I doubt the story of the broken finger, or at least that Olive was its rightful owner. Who can tell what tragic scenes may not have passed within these walls during the thirteenth and fourteenth centuries? The spectre of a nun with a bleeding finger long haunted the precincts of the abbey, and has been seen by many in former times, though I believe that her unquiet spirit is at length at rest. And I think the tale of Olive has borrowed this incident from that of a frail sister of earlier days.

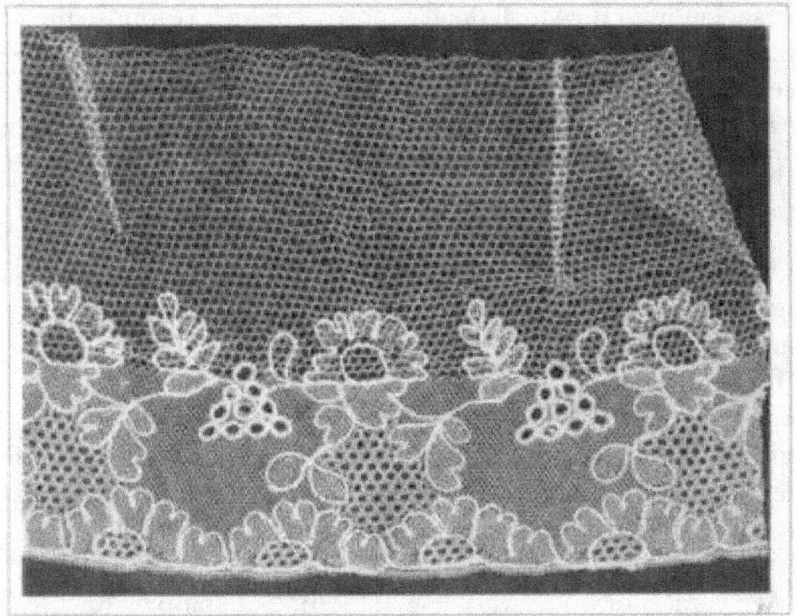

PLATE XX. LACE

As this is the first example of a *negative* image that has been introduced into this work, it may be necessary to explain, in a few words, what is meant by that expression, and wherein the difference consists.

The ordinary effect of light upon white sensitive paper is to *blacken* it. If therefore any object, as a leaf for instance, be laid upon the paper, this, by intercepting the action of the light, preserves the

39

whiteness of the paper beneath it, and accordingly when it is removed there appears the form or shadow of the leaf marked out in white upon the blackened paper; and since shadows are usually dark, and this is the reverse, it is called in the language of photography a *negative* image.

This is exemplified by the lace depicted in this plate; each copy of it being an original or negative image: that is to say, directly taken from the lace itself. Now, if instead of copying the lace we were to copy one of these negative images of it, the result would be a *positive* image of the lace: that is to say, the lace would be represented *black* upon a *white* ground. But in this secondary or positive image the representation of the small delicate threads which compose the lace would not be quite so sharp and distinct, owing to its not being taken directly from the original. In taking views of buildings, statues, portraits, &c. it is necessary to obtain a *positive* image, because the negative images of such objects are hardly intelligible, substituting light for shade, and *vice versa.*

But in copying such things as lace or leaves of plants, a negative image is perfectly allowable, black lace being as familiar to the eye as white lace, and the object being only to exhibit the pattern with accuracy.

In the commencement of the photographic art, it was a matter of great difficulty to obtain good *positive* images, because the original or negative pictures, when exposed to the sunshine, speedily grew opaque in their interior, and consequently would not yield any positive copies, or only a very few of them. But, happily, this difficulty has been long since surmounted, and the negative or original pictures now always remain transparent during the process of copying them.

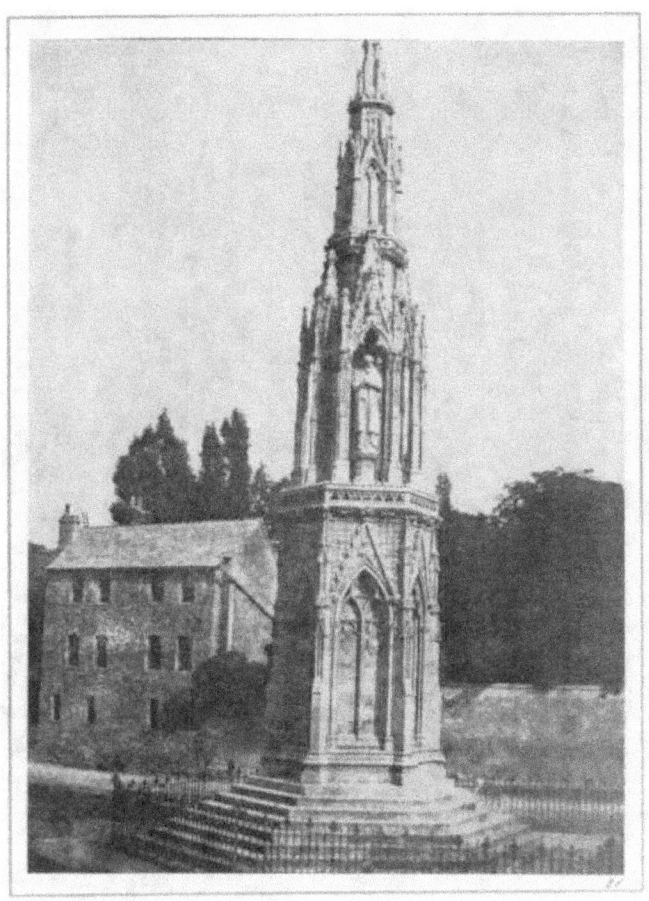

PLATE XXI. THE MARTYRS' MONUMENT

Oxford has at length, after the lapse of three centuries, raised a worthy monument to her martyred bishops, who died for the Protestant cause in Queen Mary's reign.

And we have endeavoured in this plate to represent it worthily. How far we have succeeded must be left to the judgment of the gentle Reader.

The statue seen in the picture is that of Bishop Latimer.

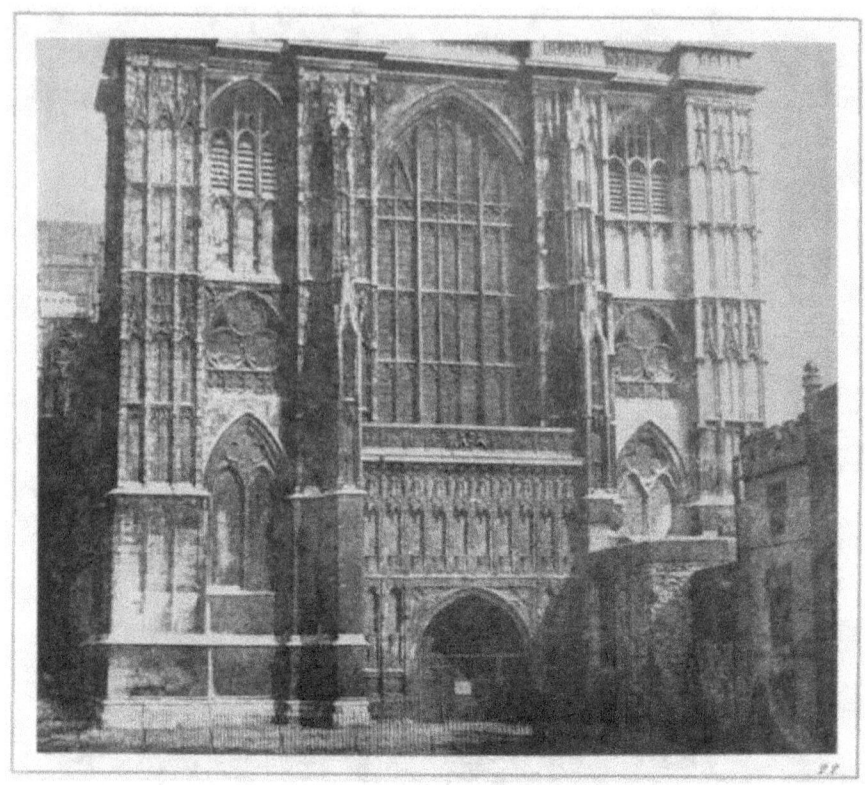

PLATE XXII. WESTMINSTER ABBEY

The stately edifices of the British Metropolis too frequently assume from the influence of our smoky atmosphere such a swarthy hue as wholly to obliterate the natural appearance of the stone of which they are constructed. This sooty covering destroys all harmony of colour, and leaves only the grandeur of form and proportions.

This picture of Westminster Abbey is an instance of it; the façade of the building being strongly and somewhat capriciously darkened by the atmospheric influence.

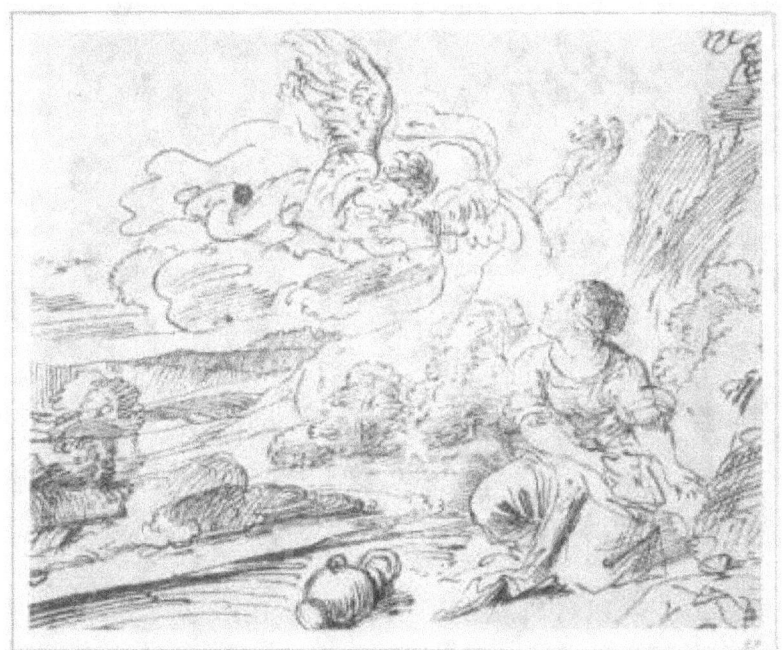

PLATE XXIII. HAGAR IN THE DESERT.

This Plate is intended to show another important application of the photographic art. Fac-similes can be made from original sketches of the old masters, and thus they may be preserved from loss, and multiplied to any extent.

This sketch of Hagar, by Francesco Mola, has been selected as a specimen. It is taken from a fac-simile executed at Munich.

The photographic copying process here offers no difficulty, being done of the natural size, by the method of superposition.

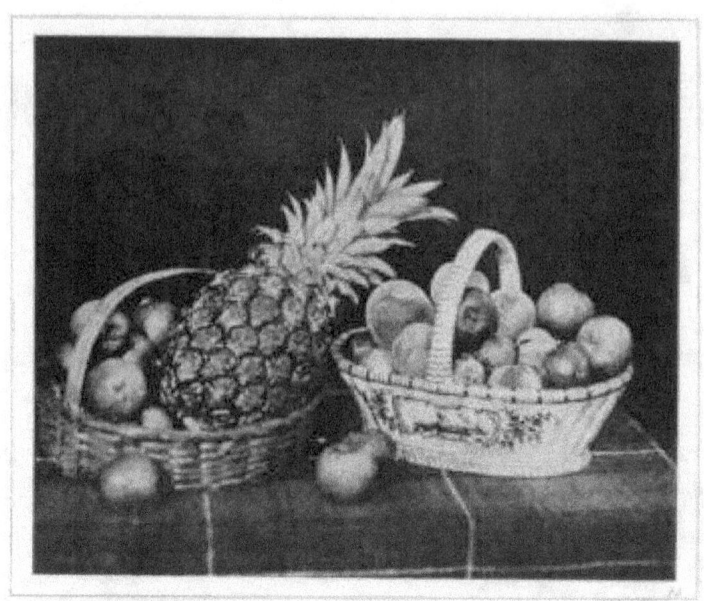

PLATE XXIV. A FRUIT PIECE.

The number of copies which can be taken from a single original photographic picture, appears to be almost unlimited, provided that every portion of iodine has been removed from the picture before the copies are made. For if any of it is left, the picture will not bear repeated copying, but gradually fades away. This arises from the chemical fact, that solar light and a minute portion of iodine, acting together (though neither of them separately), are able to decompose the oxide of silver, and to form a colourless iodide of the metal. But supposing this accident to have been guarded against, a very great number of copies can be obtained in succession, so long as great care is taken of the original picture. But being only on paper, it is exposed to various accidents; and should it be casually torn or defaced, of course no more copies can be made. A mischance of this kind having occurred to two plates in our earliest number after many copies had been taken from them, it became necessary to replace them by others; and accordingly the Camera was once more directed to the original objects themselves, and new photographic pictures obtained from them, as a source of supply for future copies. But the circumstances of light and shade and time of day, &c. not altogether corresponding to what they were on a former occasion, a slightly different but not a worse result attended the experiment.

From these remarks, however, the difference which exists will be easily accounted for.

www.ingramcontent.com/pod-product-compliance
Lightning Source LLC
Chambersburg PA
CBHW081644220526
45468CB00009B/2547